Walt Disney's Comics and Stories
No. 672 September 2006.
Published monthly by Gemstone Publishing.
© 2006 Disney Enterprises, In., except where noted.
All rights reserved. Nothing contained herein may be reproduced
without the written permission of Disney Enterprises, Inc.,
Burbank, CA, or other copyright holders.

ISBN 1-888472-39-1

Walt Disney's
Donald Duck and NEIGHBOR JONES

DEEP UN-PACT

CREATED BY CARL BARKS

AS BIRDS HEAD SOUTH AT THE FIRST SIGN OF FALL, SO DO DUCKLINGS FLEE FOR GRANDMA'S AT A FEUD'S FIRST OVERTURE!

UNCA DONALD AND NEIGHBOR JONES ARE AT IT *AGAIN!*

THIS TIME MORE *EARTH-SHATTERING* THAN BEFORE!

WHAM!

BOOM

D 2001-040

AND NEVER BEFORE HAS THERE BEEN A *SLIGHTER* RELATION BETWEEN *CAUSE* AND EFFECT!

A *COBWEB* HANGING FROM UNCA DONALD'S PRIZED PLUM TREE, WAFTED BY A SLIGHT BREEZE SO IT HOVERED OVER JONES' FLOWERBED FOR AN *INSTANT!*

THUS JONES...

⇥HEH-HEH!⇤ THIS *DEPTH CHARGE* WILL TEACH THAT DUCK A THING OR TWO ABOUT VIOLATING MY TURF!

TICK TICK TICK

ARMY SURPLUS

AND THUS DONALD!

⇥HEH-HEH!⇤ FAT OLD JONESY'S NEXT VOLLEY PROMISES TO BE CHARAC- TERISTICALLY *HEAVY- HANDED* AGAIN!

I'LL SEND IT DOWN THE SEWER PIPES! IT'S *SET* SO THAT WHEN IT PASSES UNDERNEATH DUCKIE-BOY'S HOUSE...

TICK TICK TICK

WHAT CAN *THEY* DO BESIDES *SLIGHT-LY* BLACKEN MY CEILING?

SSHHHHH

SPUT! SPUTTER DRIP

NO, WAIT! THE *HEAT* HAS SET OFF MY CEILING SPRINKLERS!

YEEK! IT DOESN'T TAKE A WOODCHUCK TO KNOW THAT POTASSIUM *IGNITES* ON CONTACT WITH *WATER!*

I'D BETTER TURN THE WATER *OFF* ALTOGETHER AND GIVE JONES NO MORE OPPORTUNITIES *THERE!*

HM... I JUST THOUGHT OF A PLACE WHERE THIS POTASSIUM CAN BE *INSTANTLY* OPERATIONAL!

CRASH!

KA-WOOSH

A HOUSE WHERE THE FLOORS ARE ALREADY *FLOODED!* *HAW! HAW!*

OW! OW! OW!

WHAT A *HOOT!* IN FACT, I ENJOYED JONES' FIERY EXIT SO MUCH THAT I'M EAGERLY AWAITING HIS *NEXT* MOVE!

CLICK!

DING DONG

THE *NERVE!* MY FORCING HIM OUT OF THE SECURE TRENCH IN HIS HOME IS NO EXCUSE FOR BRINGING THE WAR TO MY *FRONT DOOR!*

LUCKILY I KEEP A BUCKET OF *ICE WATER* READY FOR SUCH EVENTUALITIES!

IS THIS THE DUCK HOUSEHOLD, SONNY?

›WOOPS!‹

DRIP DRIP

WE'RE IN THE PROCESS OF WARNING EVERYONE WHO LIVES ON THIS STREET TO *EVACUATE!* COLONEL DUDD HERE WILL BRIEF YOU IN MORE DETAIL!

›HARUMPH!‹

A *GEOLOGICAL SCAN* SHOWS THAT A HUGE *LIVE BOMB* IS BURIED THIRTY FEET BELOW THAT FENCE, LOST DURING A TEST SHOOT IN WORLD WAR II! IF *TRIGGERED,* IT WOULD *TAKE OUT THE WHOLE BLOCK!*

YOU'RE ADVISED TO DROP EVERYTHING AND PROCEED TO THE NEAREST *EMERGENCY SHELTER!*

A **BOMB SQUAD** WILL ARRIVE SHORTLY TO DISARM IT!

YOU HAVE AN HOUR, MR. DUCK! IN THE MEANTIME, AVOID ANY ACTION THAT MIGHT CAUSE THE SLIGHTEST **VIBRATION!**

SLIGHTEST VIBRATION? HOW DO YOU LIKE THAT FOR AN **IRONIC** TWIST?!

OUR FEUD WILL HAVE TO GO ON **HIATUS!** I'M SURE JONES WILL COME TO THE SAME CONCLUSION...

...WHEN THEY TELL **HIM** ABOUT THE BOMB! WE BOTH ENJOY A GOOD FIGHT, BUT WE CERTAINLY DON'T ENTERTAIN A **DEATH WISH!**

WAK!

THE COLONEL AND THAT BUREAUCRAT ARE LEAVING **WITHOUT** WARNING JONES! HE NEVER EVEN **ANSWERED** THE FRONT DOOR!

NO WONDER! THERE HE IS AT THE **BACK DOOR**, RETURNING FROM THE ARMY SURPLUS STORE WITH A FRESH LOAD OF EXPLOSIVES!

OMIGOSH! HE **CAN'T** CONTINUE OR FEUD UNDER THE CIRCUMSTANCES! SOMEONE SHOULD **WARN** HIM!

I'LL HAVE TO DO IT!

HEY! HE'S GOT A *VIBRATING* MOBILE PHONE! MAYBE HE'LL TAKE HIS HELMET OFF TO *ANSWER* IT!

BEEP BEEP BEEP

SO I'M A *BUM*, HUH? WELL, SAMPLE *THIS!*

KA-BUMM

LISTEN, JONES! I ONLY CALLED YOU TO—DRAT! HE *HUNG UP!*

BEEP!

THERE'S OBVIOUSLY NO *COMMUNICATING* WITH HIM! SO NOW, MORE THAN *EVER*, I NEED TO *ANTICIPATE* HIS EVERY ASSAULT...

...IN ORDER TO *MUFFLE* THEIR IMPACT!

YOU'RE GETTING *SOFT*, DUCKIE, IF THE BEST YOU CAN DO IS GIVE ME AN *ITCH* THROUGH MY MOBILE PHONE!

WELL, WATCH HOW A MASTER FEUDER "REAPS" SOME *REAL VIBRATION*...

RA-TAT-TAT-TAT-TAT

...AFTER HE'S "SOWN" HIS CROP —DYNAMITE STICKS! HAR! HAR! HAR!!

THE LAWN SPRINKLERS! QUICK! THEY'LL DOUSE THE FUSES!

HAR HAR HAR! THOSE SHORT FUSES GO WITH YOUR SHORT MEMORY, DUCK!

YOU TURNED OFF THE WATER A WHILE AGO! HA HA HA!

✱ AT PAGE 3, PANEL 4!—ED.

GOODBYE, CRUEL WORLD! I'LL SOON BE LIVING ON CLOUD THIRTEEN!

PSHHHHHHHHHHH

?

HEY! WHAT GIVES?!

WHERE DID THIS PACKAGE OF ROMAN CANDLES COME FROM?

...AND WE BELIEVE THESE ARE ALL RIGHTFULLY *YOURS!*

PULL

TICK TICK

PULL

NOOOOO!!!

LATER!

OUR TIMING SEEMS TO BE ABOUT RIGHT, MEN!

YES, AND THE CRATER'S ONLY A *LITTLE* DEEPER THAN *LAST* TIME!

⇒GROAN!⇐ LOOKS LIKE THE *BIG ONE* GOT US AFTER ALL, HUH, JONE—OH! HELLO, BOYS!

⇒GROAN!⇐

WELL, WE'RE JUST RELIEVED THAT YOU AND NEIGHBOR JONES HAVE STRUCK A *TRUCE!*

CAN WE GO BACK IN NOW?

⇒AARGH!⇐ YOU'VE DONE IT *AGAIN,* DUCK...

...LEFT ANOTHER PIECE OF YOUR *JUNK* LYING AROUND TO CLUTTER UP *MY* PROPERTY!

BU... BU... BU... BU... BU...

UNCA DONALD AND NEIGHBOR JONES...⇒SIGH!⇐

THEY'RE JUST *INCAPABLE* OF *HEARING* EACH OTHER OUT!

AND WHY *SHOULDN'T* I RETURN IT TO ITS RIGHTFUL OWNER'S *SKULL?!?*

IT'S A—HELLO? DRAT! THE BATTERY'S *DEAD* AGAIN! DARN THESE MOBILE PHONES!

END

GEMSTONE PUBLISHING

presents

YOUR FAVORITE DISNEY COMICS

© 2006 Disney
Enterprises Inc.

Delivered right to your door!

We know how much you enjoy visiting your local comic shop, but wouldn't it be nice to have your favorite
Disney comics delivered to you? Subscribe today and we'll send the latest issues of your favorite comics directly to
your doorstep. And if you would still prefer to browse through the latest in comic art but aren't sure where to go,
check out the Comic Shop Locator Service at www.diamondcomics.com/csls or call 1-888-COMIC-BOOK.

WALT DISNEY'S MICKEY MOUSE

PART 3 OF 3

in love trouble

NOW, LET'S SEE! WHERE WERE WE?

HAVE YOU BEEN **AWAY?**

HAVE I B...?? UH-ULP...!

MICKEY **WAS** AWAY... ON AN ARCHAEOLOGICAL EXPEDITION WITH GOOFY!

HE ASSUMED MINNIE WOULD SPEND HIS WEEKS OF ABSENCE PINING FOR HIS RETURN!

LOOKS LIKE SHE SPENT THE TIME LANDING A NEW BOYFRIEND INSTEAD...

AH, MY BEAUTEOUS BABE!

SMACK!

SMACK!

SMACK!

SMACK!

OH, MONTY... YOU SAY THE **CUTEST** THINGS!

BUT MICKEY BOUNCES BACK!

FIRST HE MAKES SOME AS-YET-UNEXPLAINED SECRET PLANS!

NEXT HE GETS A NEW "STEADY," MILLICENT VAN GILT-MOUSE... APPARENTLY A VISITING HIGH SOCIETY BELLE!

WELL... YOU PEOPLE SEEM TO BE EVERY-WHERE!

YES, MICKEY CERTAINLY KEEPS ME ENTERTAINED! I HAVEN'T HAD AN IDLE MOMENT!

AND DOES SHE PLAY A WICKED GAME OF TENNIS!

MICKEY AND MILLICENT QUICKLY MAKE A NAME FOR THEMSELVES!

THEY'VE JUST BEEN INVITED TO AN EXCLUSIVE HIGHBROW BALL!

BUT **SO** HAS **ANOTHER** UP-AND-COMING YOUNG COUPLE...

I'D JUST LIKE TO KNOW HOW MICKEY MOUSE GOT INVITED TO THE VAN ASTOROCKS' BALL! MONTY SAYS IT'S **TERRIBLY** EXCLUSIVE!

WELL! HOW DO YOU DO, DARLING!

MY DEAR! HOW CHARMING YOU LOOK! MME. ZUZU IS REALLY WONDERFUL... I'VE **HEARD!**

YES, SHE'S VERY GOOD!

SO GLAD TO HAVE SEEN YOU!

I **SHOULD** GO IN, MYSELF, BUT I COULDN'T BE BOTHERED, REALLY!

THANK YOU... GOOD-BYE!

NOW I KNOW HOW MICKEY GOT HIS INVITATION! THAT SNIP, MILLICENT...!

...AND IF **SHE** THINKS SHE'S GOING TO OUT-SHINE **ME**...!!

GOSH, I ALMOST WISH I WASN'T GOIN' TO THAT BALL TOMORROW! SUPPOSE I PULL A SOCIAL BONER OF SOME KIND!

LET'S SEE, NOW... "AH, MRS. VAN ASTOROCKS, DELIGHTFUL PLACE YOU HAVE HERE!" HECK, NO... THAT'S TOO CORNY!

"PERFECTLY CHARMING OF YOU TO ASK ME,"... I MEAN ..."DELIGHTED TO BE HERE!"

AW, SHUCKS... SOUNDS TOO MUCH LIKE MONTY'S LINE OF TRIPE! GUESS I'LL JUST HAFTA BE MYSELF!

OH, HELLO, MILLICENT!

MICKEY, CAN YOU COME RIGHT OVER? I'VE GOT SOMETHING **PRICELESS** ON MONTY!

OH, BOY! I'M HALF-WAY THERE!

THE BIG NIGHT HAS COME! LOCAL SOCIETY GATHERS AT THE PALATIAL MANSION OF MRS. VAN ASTOROCKS FOR THE ANNUAL BALL, THE TOWN'S SNAZZIEST SOCIAL EVENT!

VERY KIND OF YOU TO INVITE ME, MRS. VAN ASTOROCKS, CONSIDERING YOU DON'T KNOW ME, AND...!

BUT I KNOW ALL **ABOUT** YOU, YOU SILLY BOY!

DON'T THINK I HAVEN'T HEARD OF YOUR EXPLOITS, YOUNG MAN! WHY, YOU EVEN SAVED THE LIFE OF A FRIEND OF MINE!

I DID? HONEST?

MICKEY IS SURPRISED TO GET A WARM RECEPTION FROM MRS VAN ASTOROCKS, WHO TELLS HIM HE ONCE SAVED THE LIFE OF A FRIEND!

NO KIDDIN'... I MEAN, REALLY? WHAT WAS HIS NAME?

PROFESSOR DUSTIBONES!

A FANTASTIC ENCOUNTER WITH CAVE-MEN, WASN'T IT? **VERY** THRILLING!

BUT NOW YOU WILL HAVE TO EXCUSE ME, WHILE I GREET THE OTHER GUESTS!

MY, ISN'T IT IMPRESSIVE? BUT, OF COURSE, **YOU'VE** BEEN HERE BEFORE!

OH, SURE! OLD STUFF TO ME!

RODAWN, DID YOU SAY? I AM AFRAID THE NAME IS **QUITE** UNFAMILIAR TO ME!

THE EVENING WEARS ON.. MUSIC AND GAIETY SPARKLE AMID THE DAZZLING SPLENDOR OF THE VAN ASTOROCKS' BALL!

A BIG ELIMINATION DANCE IS IN PROGRESS!

ARE WE SHOWIN' 'EM UP, BABE! WE'LL WIN IN A WALK!

NUMBER 23 IS ELIMINATED! PLEASE LEAVE THE FLOOR!

UH.. WHAT??

HUMPH! SMALL-TOWN JUDGES! DON'T KNOW CLASS WHEN THEY SEE IT!

ONE BY ONE THE CONTESTANTS ARE DROPPED OUT OF THE ELIMINATION DANCE, UNTIL ONLY TWO COUPLES ARE LEFT ON THE FLOOR!

CLAP! CLAP CLAP! CLAP! CLAP!

GOSH, IMAGINE ME GETTING THIS FAR! IT WAS SWELL OF YOU TO TEACH ME THAT NEW STEP!

OH, IT WAS NOTHING! YOU CAUGHT ON SO QUICKLY!

CLAP! CLAP CLAP! CLAP CLAP CLAP!!! CLAP!!

THE WINNERS! MISS MILLICENT VAN GILT-MOUSE AND MR. MICKEY MOUSE!

PHOOEY! ALL PREARRANGED!

CLAP! CLAP! CLAP! CLAP! CLAP! CLAP! CLAP! CLAP! CLAP! CLAP! CLAP!

MICKEY AND HIS PARTNER, MILLICENT, HAVE JUST WON THE ELIMINATION DANCE, THE BIGGEST EVENT OF THE SOCIETY BALL!

CLAP! CLAP! CLAP! CLAP! CLAP CLAP CLAP!!!

IS THAT MONTY BURNT UP OVER YOU STEALING HIS THUNDER!

THANKS TO YOU, PAL!

A FINE EVENING I'M HAVING! IT'S HUMILIATING!

TAKE IT EASY! I'LL SHOW UP THESE STUFFED SHIRTS YET!

THE OLD BEAN CLICKS! I'M GOIN' TO SEE THE ENTERTAINMENT CHAIRMAN!

LADIES AND GENTLEMEN! INTRODUCING MR. MONTMORENCY RODAWN, WHO WILL ENTERTAIN WITH A BRIEF DEMONSTRATION OF LEGERDEMAIN!

PAT! PAT PAT! PAT!

...PRESTO!

CLAP CLAP CLAP CLAP

MY WORD!

MEANWHILE, AT THE FRONT ENTRANCE!

HOWDY, CAP! I GOT A TELYGRAM HERE FER MONTM'RENCY RODENT!

VERY WELL, MY MAN, I SHALL DELIVER IT!

KIN YUH SING?

WHY, NO... BUT...??

THEN, MAKE WAY FER A MAN WHO KIN...IT'S A SINGIN' TELEGRAM!

In the Van Astorocks' ballroom Monty is entertaining the guests with feats of magic!

MR. RODENT, I PERSOOM?

RODAWN, STUPID... ...RODAWN! IF YOU HAVE A WIRE, GIVE IT TO ME!

HAW! HAW! I SURE WILL!

ONE MOMENT, PLEASE!

MI-MI-MI-MI...!

In the midst of Monty's success as an amateur magician, his act is interrupted by the arrival of a singing telegram!

MONTMORENCY RODENT: YOU SURE ARE IN A JAM! YOUR BOSS IS COMING HOME TONIGHT, SO TAKE IT ON THE LAM!

BRING BACK HIS AUTO AND HIS CLOTHES... RETURN HIS MONEY, TOO, FOR IF HE EVER FINDS IT OUT, IT'S JUST TOO BAD FOR YOU!

YOU'RE JUST A CHAUFFEUR HERE, YOU KNOW... GET ON THE JOB, YOU CROOK!

AND FOR THIS TIMELY WARNING... KISS MEHITABEL, THE COOK!

THAT'LL BE $1.69, COLLECT, PLEASE!

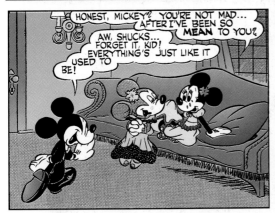

LATER!

IT'S **SO** MUCH MORE FUN GOING PLACES WITH YOU THAN IT WAS WITH MONTY!

HONEST?

YES...HE WAS SUCH A SHOW-OFF! ALWAYS DOING THINGS TO ATTRACT ATTENTION!

I KNOW! IT MUST'VE BEEN EMBARRASSING!

I HATE TO BE CONSPICUOUS, DON'T YOU?

YEH, I SURE...??!

HA! HA HA HA HA HA HA HA HA HA HA HA!!

PARDON ME, FOLKS, BUT THE ORCHESTRA STOPPED PLAYING SOME TIME AGO!

WALT DISNEY

Ye DINKY DIMPLE NIGHT SPOT

WASN'T IT A GORGEOUS EVENING? LET'S WALK HOME AND MAKE IT LAST!

BETTER TAKE A CAB, I THINK... IT LOOKS LIKE RAIN!

MICKEY MOUSE, HAVE YOU NO ROMANCE IN YOUR SOUL?

SURE, I HAVE, BUT... SAY, WHAT'RE WE STOPPING FOR?

IS MY FACE RED! I'M OUTA GAS...AN' THE STATIONS IS ALL CLOSED UP!

ROMANTIC, EH, GAL?

I STILL SAY IT'S A **GORGEOUS** EVENING!

The End

ULP!

ARE YOU A DONALDIST?

don · ald · ism \ dän'-ld-iz'-em \ *n* : the research Disney comics, and/or the fan culture that is found among Disney comics aficionados (Jon Gisle, 1973)

Go on, admit it. You like reading about comics history... but you love reading historically important comics themselves. You want a real Disney comics archival book—a thick trade paperback full of those extra-esoteric Duck and Mouse tales that just wouldn't fit in anywhere else.

You're a Donaldist! And we know where you're coming from.

Dive into the 160-page
DISNEY COMICS: 75 YEARS OF INNOVATION for:

- *Great Donald sagas by Carl Barks (a newly-restored "Race to the South Seas"), Don Rosa ("Fortune on the Rocks"), and Al Taliaferro (the semine "Donald's Nephews")*

- *Never-before-reprinted Mickey tales by Floyd Gottfredson ("Mickey Mouse Music") and Romano Scarpa ("AKA Cormorant Number Twelve")*

- *Ducks by Daan Jippes, Dick Kinney, William Van Horn, and Daniel Branca*

- *Mice by Byron Erickson, César Ferioli and Paul Murry*

- *Renato Canini's José Carioca, Gil Turner's Big Bad Wolf—and Brer Rabbit too!*

GEMSTONE PUBLISHING
presents
WALT DISNEY TREASURES VOLUME ONE
Available August 2006

(Any similarity between this book and the Disney DVDs you love to collect is purely intentional!)

WALT DISNEY
TREASURES $12
DISNEY COMICS
75 YEARS OF INNOVATION
THE OFFICIAL ANNIVERSARY BOOK
160 PAGES OF COMICS AND FEATURES
Stories First Published Internationally Between 1930 and 2004

© 2006 Disney Enterprises, Inc.

Walt Disney's Donald Duck in A Date with Daisy

WHERE HAVE YOU **BEEN,** DONALD! YOU WERE SUPPOSED TO PICK ME UP AN **HOUR** AGO! WE HAD A **DATE!**

HUH?

2003-274

I'M **TIRED** OF YOU ALWAYS STANDING ME UP! I'M **SICK** OF YOU ALWAYS BEING BROKE! AND I'VE **HAD** IT WITH YOU **FORGETTING** OUR **DATES!**

I'M SORRY! I....

SLAM!

ALL DONALD EVER DOES IS LOLL AROUND! I'LL BET HE'LL EVEN FIND A WAY TO GET OUT OF ESCORTING ME TO DUCKBURG'S GRANDE BALL!

HE'S TAKEN ME FOR GRANTED FOR THE LAST TIME! IT'S NOW OR NEVER! TIME TO TAKE A STAND!

IF I HAD *ANOTHER* BEAU...! AN ATTENTIVE, RICH GENTLEMAN WHO DOTED ON MY EVERY WHIM! *THAT* WOULD MAKE DONALD SIT UP AND TAKE NOTICE!

BUT WHO? PERFECT GUYS DON'T JUST GROW ON TREES! BUT LUCKILY, DONALD DOESN'T KNOW THAT!

AND I'LL TAKE THE ROSES, TOO! I WANT THE CARD TO READ, "DAISY, YOU ARE MY SPECIAL FLOWER"!

VERY GOOD, MADAME!

AND THEN...

PLEASE HAVE ALL THE CHOCOLATE DELIVERED TO MISS DAISY DUCK! NOW, I JUST HAVE ONE MORE STOP TO MAKE...

THINK I'LL DROP IN ON DAISY! SEE IF SHE'S COOKING UP ANYTHING GOOD FOR FUN...

AWP! WHAT'S GOING ON?

ONE SIDE, BUB!

HUH?

DAISY! WHAT GIVES?

I'VE GOT A NEW ADMIRER! ISN'T HE SWEET?

NO SOONER HAS DONALD ROUNDED THE CORNER THAN...

I DON'T BELIEVE IT! SOME LOW-DOWN CHEESE-WEASEL IS TRYING TO MUSCLE IN ON *MY* GIRL!

WHEN I GET MY HANDS ON THE CRUMB-BUM, I'LL MAKE *MINCEMEAT* OUTTA HIM!

DONALD? ARE YOU STILL HERE?

HUH? DAISY! I WAS JUST...ER... OBSERVING A RARE SAPSUCKER IN YONDER TREE! WHERE ARE YOU OFF TO? MEETING YOUR SECRET ADMIRER?

MAYBE YES! MAYBE NO!

HMMM! IF I TAG ALONG WITHOUT HER KNOWING IT, MAYBE I'LL GET THE DROP ON THAT CHISELER!

IS *THAT* THE PHILISTINE? I'LL SNAP HIM LIKE A TWIG!

MAYBE IT'S *THAT* SCHMOE! I'LL WRINKLE HIM LIKE A CHEAP SUIT!

OR IS IT *THIS* MOMMA'S BOY? I'LL FOLD HIM LIKE A....A THING YOU FOLD!

SHEESH! WHICH ONE IS IT? I NEVER REALIZED DAISY HAD DAY-TO-DAY DEALINGS WITH SO *MANY* MEN!

MY PLAN'S A *HORRIBLE* DISASTER! I'M STUCK ALL ALONE AT THE BIGGEST DANCE OF THE YEAR!

EXCUSE ME, MAC! WHO'S IN CHARGE OF THIS WING-DING?

WAIT A MINUTE! I'D KNOW THAT VOICE ANYWHERE!

I *KNEW* IT! MY DONALD'S JEALOUS! HE COULDN'T STAND THE THOUGHT OF ME BEING HERE WITH SOMEONE ELSE!

I *KNEW* YOU WOULDN'T WANT ME DANCING WITH...

HIYA, TOOTS! I JUST STOPPED BY TO RETURN THE TWO TICKETS I BOUGHT TO THIS SHINDIG!

SINCE YOU HAD *ANOTHER* DATE, I FIGURED *I* COULD LOLL AROUND HOME AND WATCH THE FIGHTS ON TV!

BWAAAH!

WHAT'S THE TROUBLE, LITTLE LADY? MAYBE I CAN HELP!

BOO HOO HOOO!

NO ONE CAN HELP ME! SOB! I'VE MADE A HUGE *MESS* OF THINGS!

THERE, THERE, MA'AM! IT CAN'T BE AS BAD AS ALL THAT!

THE ONLY ONE I'VE EVER LOVED IS DONALD! AND NOW I'VE LOST HIM FOREVER! *BWAAAAAH!*

I'LL GIVE DAISY A FEW MORE MINUTES TO STEW IN HER OWN JUICES! THAT'LL TEACH HER TO TRY TO PUT ONE OVER ON THE MASTER!

BUT I CAN'T LET HER GO ALL EVENING WITHOUT A DATE! THE POOR KID'S SUFFERED ENOUGH!

I'LL COME CLEAN WITH DAISY AND WE CAN HAVE A GOOD LAUGH WHILE WE'RE ENJOYING THE DANCE!

DAISY'S GONNA BE SURPRISED TO FIND OUT I KNEW ABOUT HER LITTLE PRANK ALL ALONG! BUT IF I KNOW MY GAL, SHE'LL GET A BIG KICK...

WAK!

HEY! BOZO! THAT'S *MY* GAL YOU'RE PAWIN'!

UNHAND HER, YOU OVERGROWN INTERLOPER, AND PUT 'EM UP! I'M ABOUT TO DROP YOU LIKE A BAD HABIT!

AND SO...

OH DONALD! YOU *DO* CARE AFTER ALL!

SURE I DO! NOW CAN YOU MOVE A LITTLE TO THE LEFT? THERE'S STILL TIME TO CATCH THE FIGHTS ON TV!

END

PANCHITO

DON' FORGET... I HAVE WAIT MONTHS FOR THEES DATE WEETH THE BEAUTIFUL CARMELINA!

THEES LOTION "FLEUR DE CACTUS" IS HAVE A MAGNIFICO BEAUTY AND I CHARGE YOU NOTHING!

ZS 44-11-12

GRACIAS! BUT YOU DON' THEENK THE SCENT IS A LEETLE **TOO** MAGNIFICO...?

A NONSENSE! SEÑORITA CARMELINA LOVES FLOWERS!

EET EEZ I, SEÑOR MARTINEZ... DON' BE AFRAID!

I THEENK I AM NOT SO SMART TO HAVE THEES HAIR LOTION...

SAFE!

NO, NO, SEÑORES! ESTOP!

FATHER! LOOK! MY BEAUTIFUL FLOWERS!

A MAGNIFICO LOTION... NO? AND I CHARGE YOU NOTHING!

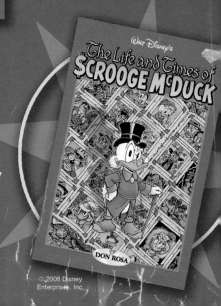

WALT DISNEY
PRESENTS

The LI'L BAD WOLF

SOON AS I GET THIS WOOD IN, I'LL HAVE TO GET POP'S BREAKFAST!

BUMP!

W WDC 121-03

WHAT TH' DING DONG IS THAT?

CLUNK!

CLUNK!

BUMP!

LI'L WOLF! IS ALL THAT NOISE NECESSARY IN TH' MIDDLE OF TH' NIGHT?

I'M SORRY, POP!

IT ISN'T THE MIDDLE OF THE NIGHT, THOUGH... THE SUN'S SHINING BRIGHT!

SALT PE[...]

AND IT'S ALMOST TIME FOR ME TO GO TO SCHOOL!

SCHOOL? BAH! YOU WENT LAST YEAR! AIN'T THAT ENOUGH?

LOOK AT ME! I DIDN'T NEED NO SCHOOLIN'! I'M A SELF-MADE MAN!

KNOCK! KNOCK! KNOCK!

OH! THAT MUST BE MY LITTLE FRIENDS I'M WALKING TO SCHOOL WITH!

SCHOOL ... **H-MPH!** I WENT T'SCHOOL ONE DAY, BUT I DIDN'T LEARN NOTHIN', SO I CAME ON HOME!

I WONDER WHAT KIDS HE WUZ TALKIN' ABOUT!

IT'S A COUPLE OF **LAMB CHOPS!** ER... I MEAN LAMB CHAPS!

I **HEERD** THERE WUZ A BAA SHEEP FAMBLY MOVED IN ... I BEEN **TRYIN'** TO FIGGER OUT HOW T'GIT TH' CRITTERS!

SOMETHIN' TELLS ME LI'L WOLF ISN'T GOIN' TO HAVE HIS LITTLE CHUMS MUCH LONGER! HEE! HEE!

THERE OUGHTA BE SOMETHIN' IN **HERE** THAT'LL HELP GET 'EM!

DISGUISES OF ALL SORTS

I NEVER HAD MUCH LUCK WITH THIS BO-PEEP OUTFIT, THOUGH!

AN' TH' DRATTED MOTHS HAVE BEEN CHEWIN' ON THIS SHEEP COSTUME!

IT'S SO MANGY NOW, I DON'T THINK IT'D FOOL **ANYBODY**!

YESSIREE! IF I'M GONNA FOOL THEM SHEEP, I CAN'T DEPEND ON A COSTUME... I GOTTA USE MY **HEAD**!

BAH! MY BEST BET IS T'HANG AROUND DURING RECESS TIME... GRAB 'EM, AN' TOSS 'EM IN THIS **BAG**!

THERE THEY ARE... BUT THERE'RE TOO MANY OTHER KIDS HANGIN' AROUND!

BAH!

HM-M... SPEAKIN' OF "**BAH**"... I BETCHA I COULD LURE 'EM INTO THIS SACK BY YELLIN' "**BAH**"!

BAA SHEEPS JEST **LOVE** TH' SOUND OF IT!

BAH! BAH! BAH!

BAA!

WAIT, LI'L LAMB! THAT SOUNDS SUSPICIOUSLY LIKE MY **POP**!

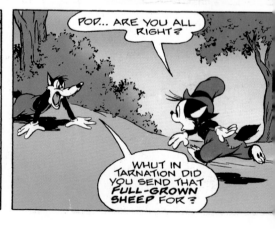

YOU DIDN'T SPECIFY WHAT **SIZE** SHEEP YOU WANTED, POP!

WELL... YOU DON'T GET TEN CENTS FER THAT **LAST** ONE!

COME T'THINK OF IT... YA DON'T GIT PAID FER **NONE** OF 'EM! THEY ALL GOT AWAY!

HEE, HEE!

I THINK MY POP HAS LEARNED HIS LESSON, FELLAS! DON'T WORRY ANYMORE!

CARNSARN IT! ALL MY BEST PLANS HAVE A WAY OF GOIN' WRONG!

I'M NOT **EVER** GOIN' TO HAVE NOTHIN' TO DO WITH SHEEPS!

BAA-A!

WH-WHY, IT'S A LI'L BLACK SHEEP! AN' HE'S **ALL** ALONE!

BAA!

HM-M... WITH NOBODY AROUND TO INTERFERE... IT'LL BE A CINCH T'GRAB THIS KID!

WELL, WELL! AN' WHY AREN'T YOU IN **SCHOOL**?

OH, I'M THE BLACK SHEEP OF MY FAMILY, AND I'M PLAYING **HOOKY** TODAY!

YEAH? WELL, YOU'VE PLAYED HOOKY FER TH' LAST TIME, SONNY!

HERE, HERE'! **WHAT'S GOIN' ON**?

WHY, MISTER TRUANT OFFICER... I WUZ JEST ASKIN' THIS LI'L OL' BLACK SHEEP WHY HE WASN'T IN SCHOOL!

WHY, TH' IGGERANT LITTLE KID DOESN'T KNOW WHAT **TWO AN' TWO** IS!

WELL...

HOW MUCH **IS** IT?

WHY, ER... UH... FIVE...ER... SIX... ER...

I THINK **YOU'D** BETTER COME ALONG WITH ME, TOO!

BAA!

BAA!

BAA!

BAH!

Walt Disney's MICKEY MOUSE in REVERTING RAPTORS

THERE THEY ARE! MY *RAPTOR* PALS! IT'S BEEN AGES SINCE I'VE SEEN 'EM!*

THANKS FER MEETIN' ME HERE TO HELP WRANGLE TH' CRITTERS, MICKEY!

*SINCE WALT DISNEY'S COMICS AND STORIES #627! -ED.

2002-190

SURE! BUT WHY'D YOU AGREE TO HIRE THEM OUT FOR A PHOTO SHOOT?!

OH, TH' RANCH DESPERATELY NEEDS TH' MONEY THEY'LL EARN!

I'M SURE THERE WON'T BE ANY PROBLEMS, BUCK! THESE FELLAHS ARE AS DOCILE AS KITTENS!

"WHEN PROFESSOR WAGSTAFF CLONED THEM HE ALTERED THEIR GENETIC CODE, MAKING 'EM HARMLESS VEGETARIANS!"

YEAH, I GUESS YOU'RE RIGHT!

C'MON! THE SHOOT'S OUT ON THE BEACH! THAT'S A BIT OF A RIDE THROUGH THE FOREST FROM HERE!

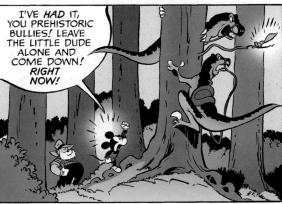

THEY ...ER... DON'T EAT MEAT!

WELL, MY NAME'S MAGGIE! I'M THE CATERER! AND THIS LITTLE BUNDLE OF ENERGY IS MY DAUGHTER, ROSIE!

I HAD TO BRING HER WITH ME TODAY 'CAUSE THE BABYSITTER TOOK SICK AT THE LAST MINUTE!

DOGGIES!

NICE MEETING YOU, ROSIE!

BUT I GUESS WE HAVE TO GET TO WORK!

SNIFF! SNIFF!

GOOD THINKIN', PAL! YUH KNOW HOW WOLVES ALWAYS LIKE TUH PICK OFF TH' YOUNG STRAGGLERS IN A HERD!

THE SHOOT COMMENCES...

THAT'S IT, GIRLS! ACT AS IF THE BEASTS ARE THREATENING! BUT BEGUILE THEM WITH YOUR FRAGRANCE!

I'M WORRIED! OUR DINOS ARE ACTING REAL EDGY! WHO KNOWS WHAT THOSE REVERTED RAPTORS MIGHT DO?

HOLY HOPPIN' MUDPUPPIES! TH' CRITTERS ARE BOLTIN'!

GROWL!

THEY'RE BARRELING TRAIGHT FOR THE ASHION MODELS!

WAIT A MINUTE! THEM COLD-BLOODED GALOOTS AIN'T AFTER TH' GIRLS! THEY'RE HEADED FER TH' *OCEAN!*

I THINK THEY'RE IN *HUNTING* MODE AGAIN! LOOK! OUT IN THE WAVES! THAT MUST BE THEIR TARGET!

A GROUP OF SEALS! FROLICKING IN THE WAVES!

THAT FLIPPERED FAMILY IS IN *BIG* TROUBLE 'LESS WE DO SOMETHIN' ABOUT IT!

COME BACK HERE, YOU TWO! STOP WHAT YOU'RE DOING THIS INSTANT!

THEY AIN'T *LISTENIN'* THIS TIME! WE GOTTA DRAG 'EM OUT WITH OUR BARE HANDS!

THINGS HAVE GOTTEN *AWFULLY* UNPREDICTABLE! I SAY WE CALL AN END TO THIS SHOOT!

RECKON YER RIGHT, MICKEY!

NOW WHAT?

HELP! MY BABY!

ROSIE! SHE *GONE*! SHE'S TODDLED OFF INTO THE FOREST!

MAGGIE! WHAT *IS* IT?

THERE ARE STEEP CLIFFS AND DEEP GULLIES IN THOSE WOODS! *ANYTHING* COULD HAPPEN TO HER!

CALM DOWN! WE'LL *FIND* HER!

'H' RAPTORS! THEY KNOW WHUT'S UP! I CAN'T HOLD ON TO 'EM!

GREEE!

DON'T WORRY! I'M IN THE SADDLE!

JUST KEEP THET KID SAFE, MICKEY!

OKAY! SO I CAN'T CONTROL THESE BEASTIES! BETTER HANG ON TIGHT AND SEE WHERE THEY TAKE ME!

WE'RE WAY OFF THE TRAIL! HOPE I HAVEN'T BITTEN OFF MORE THAN I CAN CHEW!

THE RAPTORS ARE IN THEIR ELEMENT NOW! THEY'VE SETTLED INTO HUNTING MODE! IT'S ONLY A MATTER OF TIME BEFORE THEY FIND THE CHILD! AND *THEN* WHAT?

Walt Disney's Donald Duck in Believe!

GEE, UNCA DONALD!

DO YOU HAVE TO DRIVE SO *FAST*...

...ON THIS BUMPY ROAD?

IT LOOKS LIKE *RAIN*, KIDS! IF WE'RE GOING TO HAVE A PICNIC, WE BETTER GET MOVING!

BOUNCE!

BOING!

97552

SHOOT! WE'RE NOT GONNA MAKE IT!

STOP!

SCREEEEE!!

313

WHAT'S *WRONG*? DID I HIT SOMETHING?

313

NOPE, *NOTHING!* WHAT'S *WRONG* WITH YOU, LOUIE? YOU COULDA GOTTEN US ALL *KILLED!*

LOOK! DON'T YOU SEE IT, UNCA DONALD?

WHAT!? YOU BOYS ARE STARTING TO INFURIATE ME! I DON'T SEE ANYTHING!

A *RAINBOW!*

AT THE END OF WHICH THERE'S ALWAYS...

...A POT OF *GOLD!*

1-2-3-4—

THE RAIN'S STOPPED AFTER ALL! MIGHT AS WELL HAVE OUR PICNIC RIGHT HERE!

HEY! AREN'T YOU GONNA HELP ME SET UP THIS PICNIC STUFF?

WE'LL COME BACK AND WE'LL BE *RICH!*

WE CAN CELEBRATE WITH A *PICNIC FEAST!*

GRRR! "UNCA DONALD DO THIS, UNCA DONALD DO THAT!" IT'S TIME THEY GREW UP AND STOPPED CHASING DREAMS!

I HATE TO BUST THAT CHILDISH BUBBLE OF YOURS, KIDDOS, BUT THERE AIN'T NO POT OF *GOLD* AT THE END OF THE RAINBOW!

WH-WH-WHAT?

BROTHERS, I THINK OUR UNCA'S TALKING CRAZY!

SIT DOWN OVER HERE AND RELAX, UNCA DONALD! YOU'LL SOON BE JUST FINE!

THERE'S NOTHING WRONG WITH *ME!* IT'S *YOU KIDS* WHO'VE GOT A SCREW LOOSE, BELIEVING IN A BUNCH OF *NONSENSE!*

=GASP!=

NOW I'M GONNA SET YOU *STRAIGHT!* THERE'S *NO* POINT IN BELIEVING DUMB OLD FAIRY TALES!

SURE! AND I GUESS THE *EASTER BUNNY* IS MAKE-BELIEVE TOO?

CORRECT! YOU'VE FINALLY GRASPED THE CONCEPT!

OH YEAH?

AND AT CHRISTMAS, *SANTA* AND HIS *REINDEER,* ARE JUST A *BUNCH* OF *BALONEY?*

RIGHT!

WELL, *WE* KNOW *BETTER,* DON'T WE, FELLAS?

YOU BET!

LET'S FIND OUR *GOLD!*

WE BET YOU GET *NOTHIN'* THIS CHRISTMAS, MR. KILLJOY!

OH YEAH?

Y-Y-YOU D-D-DON'T B-B-BELIEVE, D-D-DO Y-Y-YOU?

BELIEVE IN *WHAT*?!

RATTLE! RATTLE!

GREAT GROANING PUMPKINS! YOU'RE GONNA BE A *TOUGH* NUT TO CRACK!

LOOK, BUB! YOU JUST DISILLUSIONED THREE WEE, INNOCENT LADS! AN' NOW YOU GOTTA PAY THE PRICE!

BUT I ONLY TOLD 'EM THE *TRUTH!*

NOPE! YOU TRIED TO INFLUENCE THEM INTO BECOMING NON-BELIEVERS, LIKE YOURSELF! AN' THAT'S *BAD!*

SO? WHAT'S A PINT-SIZED SPUD LIKE YOU GONNA DO ABOUT IT?

FUNNY YOU SHOULD ASK!

HEY!

POOF!

WHAT'S HAPPENED AND *WHERE* ARE MY *CLOTHES?*

JUST WAIT AND SEE, DUCKY!

POOF!

WHAT'S THIS? I LOOK LIKE A *GIRL!*

POOF!

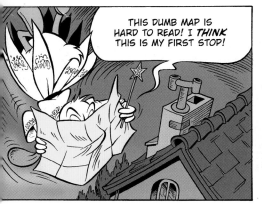

LET'S SEE IF SPIT KNOWS WHAT HE'S TALKIN' ABOUT! TAKE THE TOOTH AND... YESSIREEBOB! IT'S GONE!

POOF!

AN' HERE'S THE QUARTER! BUT IF I LEAVE IT UNDER BILLY BOB'S PILLOW, HE'LL JUST BUY CANDY THAT'LL ROT HIS NEW TOOTH!

ZZZZZZ

I'LL *KEEP IT* MYSELF! NO-ONE'LL EVER KNOW!

THREE HUNDRED QUARTERS LATER–

I'VE PREVENTED A LOTTA TOOTH DECAY BY KEEPING THE LOOT! BUT IT'S GETTING HARD TO FLY WITH ALL THESE COINS! I BETTER HEAD BACK!

CLINK!

CHINK!

ABOUT TIME, DUCKY!

I'M NEW TO THIS FAIRY BUSINESS!

CLINK!

CHINK!

CHINK!

SAY! YOU LOOK KINDA *LUMPY!*

UMM...THE KIDS LEFT ME LOTSA *TREATS...*

KIDS LEAVE *SANTA* TREATS, DUCKY! WHATCHA GOT STUFFED UNDER YOUR GOWN?

HEY! LEGGO!

CHING!

CLINK!

CLINK!

FOR *SHAME!* I'VE SEEN SOME *LOUSY* TOOTH FAIRIES IN MY TIME, BUT YOU'RE THE WORST! GET BACK AND *RETURN* EVERY CENT!